MEDIA &
THE NEWS

by

Holly Duhig

CRABTREE
PUBLISHING COMPANY
WWW.CRABTREEBOOKS.COM

CRABTREE
PUBLISHING COMPANY
WWW.CRABTREEBOOKS.COM

Published in Canada
Crabtree Publishing
616 Welland Avenue
St. Catharines, ON
L2M 5V6

Published in the United States
Crabtree Publishing
PMB 59051
350 Fifth Ave, 59th Floor
New York, NY 10118

Published in 2019 by Crabtree Publishing Company

First Published by Book Life in 2018
Copyright © 2018 Book Life

Author: Holly Duhig

Editors: Madeline Tyler, Janine Deschenes

Design: Danielle Rippengill

Proofreader: Melissa Boyce

Print and production coordinator:
Katherine Berti

All facts, statistics, web addresses and URLs in this book were verified as valid and accurate at time of writing. No responsibility for any changes to external websites or references can be accepted by either the author or publisher.

Printed in the U.S.A./122018/CG20181005

Photographs
Shutterstock
    BigTunaOnline: p. 22
    Denys Prykhodov: p. 7 (center left, bottom right)
    drserg: p. 7 (top right)
    Featureflash Photo Agency: p. 8 (center left), 25 (left), 27 (left)
    Gregory Reed: p. 13
    Jaguar PS: p. 27 (right)
    Lawrey: p. 2
    Luciano Mortula - LGM: p. 10 (bottom)
    Pres Panayotov: p. 4 (far bottom right)
    Roman Nerud: p. 15 (top right)
    Thinglass: p. 20
    Twocoms: p. 29
Wikimedia Commons
    Cecil Beaton: p. 6 (bottom right)
    De Larmessin: p. 6 (top right)
    Gage Skidmore from Peoria, AZ, United States of America: p. 9 (bottom)
    Massachusetts Historical Society: p. 6 (center left)
All other images by Shutterstock

Library and Archives Canada Cataloguing in Publication

Duhig, Holly, author
    Media and the news / Holly Duhig.

(Our values)
Includes index.
Issued in print and electronic formats.
ISBN 978-0-7787-5434-3 (hardcover).--
ISBN 978-0-7787-5497-8 (softcover).--ISBN 978-1-4271-2225-4 (HTML)

    1. Media literacy--Juvenile literature. 2. Journalism--Juvenile literature. 3. Mass media--Technological innovations--Juvenile literature. 4. Fake news--Juvenile literature. I. Title.

P96.M4D84 2018   j302.23   C2018-905499-9
                                              C2018-905500-6

Library of Congress Cataloging-in-Publication Data

Available at the Library of Congress

CONTENTS

Words that are **boldfaced** can be found in the glossary on page 31.

WHAT IS THE MEDIA?

When people talk about the media, they are talking about all the forms of **mass communication** that we use to connect with others and to pass information between people. Media is a means of gaining and sharing knowledge. It can entertain, inform, connect, and influence people. From social media to billboards, there are many different media types. Some types of media allow us to share our ideas and creativity with others, while other types of media keep us up to date about events happening around us.

MOVIES

MUSIC

TELEVISION

VIDEO GAMES

BOOKS

NEWSPAPERS AND MAGAZINES

RADIO

ADVERTISEMENTS

Social media is a type of media that you probably use every day. It refers to websites and applications (apps) that we use to connect with friends and family, and to follow people we admire such as celebrities. Facebook, Twitter, Instagram, YouTube, and Snapchat are all examples of social media. It's also common to see other kinds of media, such as **advertisements**, music, and news articles, shared on social media **feeds**.

WHAT IS THE NEWS?

The news refers to new information about recent events or changes in the world, which is communicated to us using media. News can be local, which means it focuses on events happening in your local area; national, meaning it focuses on things happening in your country; or international, which means it reports on events happening all over the globe. The news **industry** is huge, and is made up of many different media organizations. These are companies that might own multiple news **outlets**.

BREAKING NEWS

PEOPLE WHO WRITE ABOUT AND REPORT THE NEWS ARE CALLED JOURNALISTS.

Advances in technology mean that we have access to news all of the time. We might hear it on the radio on the way to school, see it on the TV in the evening, or read it on our smartphones at any time of day. Today, much of our news is international because the Internet is able to connect us to other countries. International news is important because we are all part of a **global community**. Events and issues that happen in other countries still affect us. Some issues reported in the news, such as climate change, affect everyone on Earth.

TIMELINE OF THE MEDIA

15th Century—Johannes Gutenberg invents the **printing press**, which allows books to be produced in large numbers. This means more and more people have access to books.

17th Century—Newspapers are **circulated** in many European countries. The first newspaper in the United States is published in 1690. In Canada, the first newspaper was published in 1752.

PUBLICK OCCURRENCES

FIRST AMERICAN NEWSPAPER

1895—The world's first **commercial** film screening takes place at the Grand Café in Paris.

1906—On December 24, 1906, the first entertainment and music radio **broadcast** is transmitted to the public from Brant Rock, Massachusetts.

1953—Broadcast on the new medium of television, the coronation of Queen Elizabeth II was watched by an estimated 277 million people worldwide. For some, it was their first time watching television.

CORONATION OF ELIZABETH II

1990—Tim Berners-Lee invents the World Wide Web, which allows information to be shared among people all over the world.

TIM BERNERS-LEE

1999—One of the first popular instant messaging sites, Windows Live Messenger (MSN), is launched.

2003—Social networking sites take off, and Myspace, one of the most popular social networks at the time, is launched.

2004—Facebook, the social networking site founded by Mark Zuckerberg, is launched. To this day, it is still the most popular social network.

2006—Twitter is launched.

2005—The video-sharing service YouTube is launched.

2017—Social media as a source for news increases. A study by Pew Research Center shows that 67 percent of Americans get at least some of their news from social media. 42 percent of Canadians check social media for news at least once per day.

PRODUCING MEDIA

Many different people are involved in producing the media you see each day. It's important to remember that the media you see has been created from the point of view of the people who created it. Every piece of media has a point of view. These are some of the people involved in creating different kinds of media.

Journalist: Journalists are people who report on the daily news or issues that affect people around the world. Journalists might write articles for newspapers, magazines, and websites. They might also work as reporters on television networks. Journalists usually specialize in certain topics. For example, a sports journalist covers sports games, and a foreign correspondent reports on events happening in other countries.

SAMUEL L. JACKSON IS AN ACTOR WHO HAS APPEARED IN OVER 100 FILMS INCLUDING *CAPTAIN AMERICA* AND *JURASSIC PARK*.

Actor: Actors take on the roles of characters in television shows, movies, and plays. Actors usually have to learn a script from memory so that, when they need to, they will be able to perform their role. Actors also learn their characters inside and out, so they can convince the audience of their role.

Writer: Writers create the material that you see in the media. They might write books or articles for magazines. They might write storylines or scripts for TV shows and films. These writers are called screenwriters. They might write the scripts or taglines you see on news shows and advertisements.

Producer: Producers are the people who finance and manage the production of a TV show, movie, news broadcast, or other media. They are often in control of who is hired in other roles in media and how they will work to create the project. Producers might work for a production company or work independently. They are in control of the whole project.

Director: A director is someone whose job it is to direct how a movie or TV show is made. They supervise the **cast** and **technical crew** of a film. It is also the director's job to have a creative "vision" of how they want a film to look, and to make sure that vision is met by overseeing everything from set design and lighting to camera angles and editing. When you watch a movie or TV show, you are likely seeing the director's point of view.

Editor: Editors work in a range of mediums, from print media to movies and TV. Editors might check written words such as books for accuracy, clarity, and correct spelling and grammar. In film-making and TV show production, an editor goes through all of the camera footage and pieces it together into an understandable storyline. They have a lot of influence over the point of view of a movie or show.

A PRODUCTION COMPANY OR PUBLISHER CONTROLS THE KIND OF MEDIA YOU SEE. THEY CHOOSE WHICH MOVIES TO PRODUCE OR WHICH BOOKS TO SELL. REMEMBER THAT THE INFORMATION YOU SEE IS CHOSEN AND CONTROLLED BY THESE COMPANIES.

PATTY JENKINS WAS THE DIRECTOR OF THE FILM *WONDER WOMAN*.

MEDIA LITERACY

With all the media around us every day, it's important to know strategies that can help us understand the messages it sends. Knowing how to identify and understand different media messages means that you have media literacy skills. Media literacy is a term that has been used for many years. It helps you identify different types of media, critically examine their messages, and draw conclusions about the information you're presented with. A person who is media literate never takes messages at **face value**. They always question what they read, see, or hear to identify the real message behind the media.

Having media literacy skills means that you can seek out and understand information about issues that interest you. If you want to learn more about a current issue like the debate over oil pipelines, for example, you know how to find credible sources of information and sift through that information to find meaning. It also means you know how to protect yourself against targeted or false advertising, scams, or untrue information.

HAVING MEDIA LITERACY SKILLS HELPS YOU BE A SMART, INFORMED CONSUMER OF MEDIA AND THE PRODUCTS IT ADVERTISES.

HOW DOES THE MEDIA INFLUENCE HOW YOU SEE CERTAIN GROUPS OF PEOPLE? FOR EXAMPLE, WHEN YOU VIEW NEWS OR ENTERTAINMENT MEDIA, WHO DO YOU USUALLY SEE IN PROFESSIONAL WORKPLACE ROLES? DO YOU OFTEN SEE WOMEN, OR PEOPLE WHO HAVE PHYSICAL DISABILITIES IN THESE ROLES?

A STRONG INFLUENCE

The messages that different kinds of media send have a stronger impact on you and your beliefs than you might realize. Every type of media tells a story. A work of fiction might weave a tale with fantasy characters, and a movie might introduce you to the life of a fictional character. But nonfiction media also tells stories. A news report tells you the story of an event. A music video presents a certain image to viewers. All of the people you see in media play a role that reinforces that story. And every story has a certain point of view that is then transferred to the consumer of that media. The stories told and the roles played in media affect how you see it— and how you see the world around you. Consider how your beliefs about certain people or issues are shaped by how they are portrayed in media. Being media literate means you can see how the media influences your perceptions, and then think for yourself.

THE PEOPLE WHO OWN THE MEDIA—USUALLY THE HEADS OF VERY LARGE CORPORATIONS— DECIDE HOW THINGS ARE PRESENTED TO YOU, AND THEREFORE INFLUENCE HOW YOU SEE THINGS.

11

IDENTIFYING BIAS

An important part of being media literate is the ability to recognize and identify **bias** in media. Everyone has bias. It is a feeling or opinion that might show a preference or dislike for something. It often means that we have a **predetermined** belief about something. Bias is not always a negative thing. Everyone has opinions and beliefs. However, bias can be harmful when it perpetuates untrue **stereotypes** or supports **discriminatory** worldviews.

"THIS CHAIR IS RED" IS A FACTUAL STATEMENT, WITH NO BIAS. HOWEVER, THE STATEMENT "THIS IS A NICE CHAIR" IS AN OPINION THAT MAY INCLUDE SOME BIAS. IS THE SPEAKER'S FAVORITE COLOR RED, FOR EXAMPLE, OR DID A FRIEND OF THEIRS DESIGN THE CHAIR?

It is important to be aware of bias in the news because the way news is reported can affect your own opinions. If something is reported with an existing bias, this bias transfers over to how viewers or readers see the subject. Begin to identify bias by recognizing whether a statement is fact or opinion. A fact can be proven true or false, whereas an opinion is an expression of someone's feelings and cannot be proved to be right or wrong.

Being aware of bias in media can help you form your own opinions and perceptions about the information you read and view. You should also try to identify your own bias. As a consumer of media, you bring your own opinions to a story. Your opinions affect how you perceive it. For example, you may have heard or seen a news story about NFL players kneeling during the national anthem. From the players' perspective, kneeling is a way of showing protest against the oppression of black and other nonwhite people in America. A person who agrees that nonwhite people are treated unfairly might see kneeling as a peaceful act of protest, and view the news story positively. However, a person who disagrees might see kneeling as **unpatriotic**. They will have a negative view of that same news story. This also goes for the media companies, and the reporters, who broadcast the story. Their own views are likely to affect whether they present the players' actions in a positive or negative light. Recognizing this bias can help you to avoid being swayed by bias in how media stories are presented—and your own bias in how you interpret those stories.

MEDIA LITERACY CAN HELP YOU FOCUS ON THE FACTS OF A STORY AND FORM YOUR OWN OPINIONS.

Sometimes, bias is present in media stories accidentally, because everyone involved in creating media has their own opinions and views. Other times, bias is present in media stories on purpose, and is meant to sway the audience to believe a certain thing. For example, if an online news website receives advertising money from an oil company, they may present stories about oil pipelines in a positive light, without focus on the possible negative outcomes of the pipelines. One way you can be media literate is to pay attention to the advertisements on news websites and stations, and to do research about who owns different news companies.

CENSORSHIP IN THE MEDIA

According to the **United Nations**' Universal Declaration of Human Rights (UDHR), every person on Earth has the right to free speech. This means that they can express their thoughts and ideas without other people trying to stop them—as long as their speech does not harm others (called **hate speech**, **slander**, or **libel**). Despite this right, the media in many countries around the world is limited and controlled by governments or by large organizations. Placing limits on what sorts of things can be reported in the news, or shown in the media, is called censorship.

COUNTRIES LIKE NORWAY, SWEDEN, AND FINLAND HAVE THE LEAST RESTRICTED PRESS, WHILE COUNTRIES LIKE NORTH KOREA AND SAUDI ARABIA HAVE THE MOST RESTRICTED PRESS. IN THOSE COUNTRIES, THE GOVERNMENT CONTROLS MUCH OF WHAT CITIZENS ARE ALLOWED TO SEE IN THE MEDIA.

The United States, Canada, the United Kingdom, and many European countries have what is called "free press." This means that news and media outlets are allowed to express any opinion they want, and are free to criticize the government. However, some countries don't have free press. North Korea is an example of a country where the media is heavily censored in order to make people think a certain way. A lot of the media in North Korea is considered propaganda. This means that it promotes only the viewpoint that supports the government.

Sometimes censorship can be a good thing. Age **restrictions** on films and games are generally agreed upon because they prevent young children from seeing things that might upset them. Hateful and harmful opinions should sometimes be censored to protect others. However, when most facts and opinions are censored in the media and the news, it can be used to influence people. Seeing only one viewpoint in the news limits how viewers and consumers are able to form their own opinions. This can be dangerous because it allows those who are in control of the media to control how a population thinks.

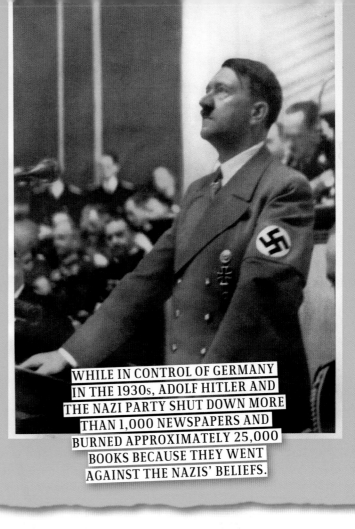

WHILE IN CONTROL OF GERMANY IN THE 1930s, ADOLF HITLER AND THE NAZI PARTY SHUT DOWN MORE THAN 1,000 NEWSPAPERS AND BURNED APPROXIMATELY 25,000 BOOKS BECAUSE THEY WENT AGAINST THE NAZIS' BELIEFS.

WE NEED A FREE PRESS THAT SHOWS A RANGE OF OPINIONS AND POLITICAL VIEWS SO THAT PEOPLE CAN CHOOSE WHAT THEY BELIEVE.

Having a free, uncensored press is an extremely important feature of a free and **democratic** society. In a democratic society, people vote for leaders who will represent their interests in government. News media gives voters the information they need to make informed choices about voting. If a certain political viewpoint is censored in the media, voters cannot reach an informed decision. This means that without a free press, a society is not truly democratic.

IS IT FAKE NEWS?

You have probably heard or read the terms "fake news" and "alternative facts" in the print, television, and online media you see each day. The reality is that there is a lot of misinformation out there. Fake news stories are news stories that are not true. Other stories have misinformation such as skewed statistics, exaggerated facts, and biased writing.

BECAUSE ANYONE CAN POST INFORMATION ONLINE, THE INTERNET IS A COMMON PLACE FOR MISINFORMATION AND FAKE NEWS.

Misinformation is often used purposely to influence readers or to get viewers to agree with a certain perspective. Statistics might be presented in a misleading way so that they support a certain side of an issue. Facts that go against a certain view could be left out. Other facts could be falsely created or exaggerated to support a viewpoint.

News stories might be falsely created to make people believe something about a group or an issue. Fake news stories are also written to make money. Some online stories are written with false or misleading headlines or facts to get people to click on them or share them. Clicks and shares can make the website money.

Search engines, such as Google, and social media sites, such as Facebook and Twitter, feature news stories written by people on many different websites. We might feel that we can trust news stories featured on search engines we rely on, or posted by people whom we trust. However, search engines and social media sites do not **filter** the news stories they feature by whether they are valid. To be valid means to be true or accurate. The stories featured are chosen by **algorithms** rather than real people. This means no one is checking how trustworthy these websites are—and we do not know who is writing them. When others share the stories, they may not realize the story contained misinformation. Make sure you check every story you click on for its validity.

TRY TO FIND OUT IF THE AUTHOR OF AN ARTICLE IS EDUCATED IN THE TOPIC THEY HAVE WRITTEN ABOUT.

When you read a news story or any other information online, check its validity by examining the source. The source is where the article originally came from. Who wrote the article, and what organization did they work for? Are they qualified to write about the topic they have written about? Do you recognize the website on which the article or information was posted?

IDENTIFYING FAKE NEWS

Many fake news stories have typical features or topics. Knowing what to look for can help you identify whether an article you are reading is false. Fake news stories are often clickbait. This means their headlines announce something shocking, frightening, or too good to be true. Many fake news articles are about:

- A shocking scientific discovery or miracle cure for a disease
- A scandal or terrible crime
- Something that makes you feel angry or frightened, or a prediction for a horrible disaster

If you read a story about a scandal, crime, or disaster that seems unreal, check whether the story is being reported elsewhere. If it is not reported on another credible site, it may be fake. Fake news stories often play on people's emotions to influence them to share the article with others. Before sharing any article, make sure that it is valid.

A FAKE NEWS ARTICLE OFTEN USES VERY EMOTIONAL LANGUAGE TO MAKE YOU ANGRY OR SCARED ENOUGH TO SHARE IT WITH OTHERS.

ALIEN LIFE

MISINFORMATION MEANT TO SPREAD FEAR CAN MAKE US DISTRUSTING OF OTHER PEOPLE IN OUR COMMUNITIES. REMEMBER TO LEARN ABOUT AN ISSUE FROM ALL PERSPECTIVES SO THAT WE DO NOT WRONGLY BLAME FEAR ON OTHERS.

Being able to evaluate the validity of the media you read and hear is an extremely important part of being media literate. You should always check for signs of misinformation when you encounter new articles. Here are some questions that you can ask yourself or steps that you can take when you read information online.

- Have you heard of the website or organization that published the information?
- Who is the author of the story? Are they qualified to write about that topic? Have they written other articles on the topic?

- Check the web address to make sure it is legitimate, and that it's not a site trying to mimic a credible source. Check that the address ends in a credible suffix such as .gov, .org, or .edu. These usually come from legitimate organizations such as governments, organizations, or schools.
- When was the article published? If it is not current, the information may be out of date or been proven wrong.
- Have you heard the story reported elsewhere? Has it been on the TV or radio?
- What is the purpose of the story? Is it meant to shock, scare, anger, or excite an audience?

ADVERTISING

Advertisements are another kind of media that are meant to influence how people think and behave. You see, hear, and read them every day on smartphones, televisions, social media feeds, billboards, or radio stations. Part of media literacy is recognizing how advertisements work to catch your attention and sell you a product. That way, you can sift through all of the advertisements for different products, and make informed choices about your purchasing power. You can also identify when an advertisement might be using misleading or **manipulative** tactics to sell a product.

IN ONE DAY WE MIGHT SEE BETWEEN 250 TO 3,500 ADVERTISEMENTS DEPENDING ON WHO WE ARE AND WHERE WE LIVE. HOWEVER, A LOT OF THE TIME WE DON'T NOTICE THEM AT ALL.

Advertisements are important to companies because they gather consumers for the products they produce. They also fund things such as TV shows and YouTube channels, because advertisers pay money to TV channels and YouTube **vloggers** to run ads on those mediums. Advertisements have to follow certain standards, regulated by the Federal Trade Commission in the United States and by Advertising Standards Canada. Advertisers are not allowed to lie to the public or advertise certain products to children.

GET CRITICAL

Being media literate means you can think critically about the advertisements you see and understand the **implied** messages behind them. For example, a group of smiling friends in an ad for a clothing company sends the message that you should buy the clothing. However, the implied message is that if you wear the clothing, you will be happy and social too.

ADVERTISEMENTS OFTEN SELL A CERTAIN DESIRABLE "LIFESTYLE," OR WAY OF LIVING. THEY TRY TO CONVINCE CONSUMERS THAT BUYING THE PRODUCT MEANS THEY ARE PART OF THAT LIFESTYLE. IMAGINE THE IMAGE BELOW BEING USED FOR A VEHICLE ADVERTISEMENT. WHAT KIND OF LIFESTYLE IS IT SELLING?

BEING IN THE KNOW

Part of being media literate—and being a smart consumer—is the ability to recognize when you are being advertised to. As more and more advertising moves online, it's important to be able to recognize online ads. For example, when you use a search engine to find a website or to ask a question, the first few results are usually advertisements relating to what you searched for. This is because companies pay for search engines like Google to advertise them at the top of their search results page. These advertisements look like normal search results, but they usually have something underneath them saying "ad" or "sponsored" to show that it is an ad.

SOCIAL MEDIA SITES LIKE FACEBOOK, INSTAGRAM, AND TWITTER SHOW YOU ADVERTISEMENTS IN YOUR NEWSFEED. HOWEVER, THERE IS SOMETHING THAT TELLS YOU THAT WHAT YOU ARE SEEING IS AN AD.

A lot of the advertising you encounter daily—maybe without realizing it—is on social media. Some clear examples are the ads that run before YouTube videos or that feature along the sides of articles you read. Instagram influencers and YouTube vloggers might promote certain products in their posts and videos, too. They are usually sponsored, or paid by the companies to feature these products. In most of these cases, the person making the ad needs to state to viewers that their post is an ad. This is because at first, many people did not know that they were being advertised to when the people they follow posted product recommendations. Now, this kind of advertising is very clear.

Some online advertisements are harder to identify. Many websites use cookies to advertise to you. Cookies are files that are downloaded onto your computer when you visit certain websites. They contain a record of your activity while on that site. They might record what links you click, how long you spend on the site and what sorts of things you look at. This means that, when you next visit that website, the site can show you things that it thinks you might like to see. Cookies can make using the site easier, but they can also be used to "retarget" you with advertisements when you are on other sites. By "tagging" your browser with a cookie, they can show you ads for the things you looked at on their website, even when you are on a different website.

#AD

YOUTUBE HAS A RULE STATING THAT YOUTUBERS MUST EITHER CLEARLY TELL THEIR VIEWERS THAT THEY ARE BEING SPONSORED, OR PUT "AD" IN THE TITLE OF THE VIDEO.

MEDIA AND SELF-IDENTITY

Your self-identity is how you see yourself. It can include your personal qualities, the groups to which you belong, and your body image. Media such as movies, TV shows, magazines, and even advertisements can have a huge effect on our self-identity. When certain types of people are more commonly shown in media, we might believe that is how all people should look or behave. If our bodies, interests, and personal qualities don't fit with what the media tells us is "normal," we might believe that we need to change who we are.

Comparing ourselves to the images we see in the media can have a negative effect on our body image. Our body image is what we think about our physical appearance when we look in the mirror. Studies have shown that people's exposure to images of seemingly perfect-looking celebrities in the media can cause us to have a negative body image. However, the media is often guilty of editing the images of people to make them appear closer to widely held beliefs about what is beautiful or attractive. They might make people look slimmer, taller, and free of blemishes. Social media is another area where we might see unrealistic representations of how people look. Apps such as Instagram allow you to edit pictures before posting them. When we compare ourselves to edited pictures on social media, this can also negatively affect our body image.

Many celebrities have spoken out publicly about how their appearances have been edited in the media without their **consent**. Meghan Trainor's biggest hit single "All About That Bass" includes lyrics that criticize magazines for editing photos. Despite this, when the video for her song "Me Too" came out, she realized that it had been edited to make her look slimmer, so she took the video down. She wrote on social media to express her disappointment, stating that she would leave the video down until the mistake was fixed. She later uploaded an unedited version of the video.

MEGHAN TRAINOR

BEING AWARE THAT WHAT WE SEE IN THE MEDIA ISN'T ALWAYS REAL CAN HELP US FEEL MORE CONFIDENT IN OUR OWN SKIN.

Our self-identity is made up of more than how we look. Things such as our interests, qualities, friends, and family also make up who we are. How we view our identity is also affected by the kinds of social groups, interests, and other qualities we commonly see featured in media. Have you noticed if teens in the media you consume share any interests with you? Do you commonly see certain types of friend groups or family units? Remember that the media does not always reflect the diversity of our world. If you don't see your interests and personal qualities in media, it doesn't mean they are not normal.

DIVERSITY IN MEDIA

Our communities are made up of people of all different ages, genders, body types, races, abilities, interests, backgrounds, and ethnicities. We live in societies full of diversity! However, the media, especially film and television, does not always reflect this diversity. The people we see in media influence how we see ourselves and those around us. If people of just a few races, backgrounds, and abilities are featured in media, we may falsely believe that those kinds of people are normal—and those that are different do not belong. It's important to think critically about the types of people you see in media. Are women featured in professional roles? Are most women mothers? Do you see single fathers or successful immigrants? Do you see people of different abilities and races in prominent roles? What about same-sex couples or transgender characters? How are they portrayed, or shown?

Whitewashing is a phenomenon in media in which white people are featured more often, and in a more positive light, than nonwhite people. Often it means that the physical features of white people, such as straight hair and light skin, are shown as being more beautiful or attractive than other features. Many products, such as hair-smoothing shampoo or skin-lightening cream, are advertised to enhance "white" features. It can also mean that white actors are more commonly used in media. This means that movies, TV shows, advertisements, and other media do not reflect racial diversity.

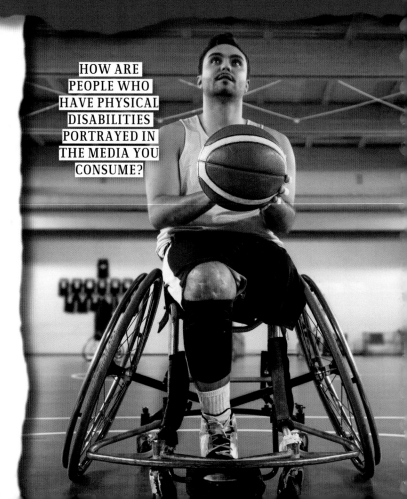

HOW ARE PEOPLE WHO HAVE PHYSICAL DISABILITIES PORTRAYED IN THE MEDIA YOU CONSUME?

Hollywood has a history of whitewashing, in which white actors are hired to play characters originally written as nonwhite, white professionals are given more opportunities, and white actors are celebrated more often than nonwhite actors. In 2016, all 20 of the nominees for the best actor and actress awards at the Academy Awards, or Oscars, were white. The hashtag #OscarsSoWhite was started on social media to get people talking about whether the Oscars **disproportionately** awarded white actors over those who are nonwhite. Even former US president Barack Obama got involved in the conversation, saying "I think when everybody's story is told, then that makes for better art. [...] It makes everybody feel part of one American family." Obama's words are important. When some people's stories are not told in media, they may feel like outsiders; as if they do not belong in the society in which they live.

BEST ACTOR AND ACTRESS WINNERS, OSCARS 2017

THE ACADEMY AWARDS IS AN AWARDS CEREMONY THAT CELEBRATES ACHIEVEMENTS IN THE FILM INDUSTRY.

The campaign for more diversity meant that the organizers behind the Oscars agreed to increase diversity in their membership. The next Oscars ceremony in 2017 featured much more diversity in its nominees. The Oscar for Best Picture that year went to the film *Moonlight*, which had a cast made up entirely of black actors and actresses. Though there were some positive changes, ensuring that the media gives equal opportunity to all people—and represents the diversity of our world—is an ongoing issue. We should continue to speak out and demand that the media we consume reflects all people's experiences.

MEDIA ACTIVISM

One of the most amazing things about social media is its ability to bring about change. More and more of our news is international, which means we hear about things happening all over the world. This means reports of war, natural disasters, and **humanitarian crises** reach people all around the world, and some of these people might be able to help.

FLOODING CAUSED BY HURRICANE HARVEY

EVEN THE SOCIAL MEDIA APP SNAPCHAT, WHICH HAD BEEN CRITICIZED FOR ITS MAPS FEATURE WHERE YOU COULD FIND THE LOCATION OF YOUR FRIENDS, HELPED IN THE WAKE OF HURRICANE HARVEY.

In 2017, Hurricane Harvey hit Texas in the United States. It destroyed nearly 135,000 homes and cost a lot of money to clean up. It was the second-most expensive hurricane in the US since 1900. Hurricane Harvey was reported worldwide in traditional media, and disaster relief charities also took to social media to ask for donations. Social media also proved to be a lifeline for some. When emergency phone lines were **congested**, people turned to social media for help. One Twitter account, @HarveyRescue, even set up a Google document where people who needed rescuing could enter their location and request help.

Occasionally, campaigns for change go **viral** on social media. In 2017 and 2018, the #MeToo movement went viral on Twitter. It raised awareness about sexual assault and harassment. It encouraged people to speak out about their experiences. The huge numbers of people using the hashtag showed how widespread the issue is. #BlackLivesMatter is another example of a social media campaign that went viral. It raised awareness about racism against black people, especially highlighting instances of police brutality against them. Viral social media messages are also used to show support for causes. Following disasters or violent attacks, people often post their support for victims and survivors.

THE VIRAL ALS ICE BUCKET CHALLENGE RAISED OVER $115 MILLION FOR THE ALS ASSOCIATION. IT ALSO BROUGHT AWARENESS OF THE DISEASE TO MANY PEOPLE AROUND THE WORLD.

"SLACKTIVISM"

Some people criticize the effect social media has had on activism. They state that the majority of social media users simply post about issues, instead of actively working to create change. Sometimes, issues go "viral" on social media, but they are not resolved in the real world. Posting on social media gives people a way to get involved, but with very little real effort. People call this phenomenon "slacktivism."

THINK ABOUT IT

 1 Do you watch or read the news? What was the last news story you heard that caught your attention? Why did that story catch your eye?

 **2** Think about all of the media you consumed today—even in this book. What kinds of people did you see featured most often? Do you feel the media you saw today reflected the diversity of the world we live in? Why or why not? Why is diversity in media important?

 **3** Have you seen any examples of social media activism in your life? How did they contribute to the cause? Do you feel social media activism is effective?

 4 Refer back to the strategies on page 19 that help identify misinformation and fake news. Have you used any of these strategies in the past? Can you think of any other strategies that would be useful in identifying misinformation? Share your strategies with a peer.

GLOSSARY

advertisements Media meant to sell something

algorithms A process or set of rules that a computer follows to make calculations

bias A feeling or opinion that may show a preference or preconceived belief

broadcast Transmission of radio or television program

browser An application used to search for and view websites

cast The actors in a movie, TV show, or play

circulated Widely distributed and sold

commercial Able to make a profit

congested Overcrowded or clogged up

consent Another word for having someone's permission

consumer A buyer of goods and services

credible Believable, trustworthy

democratic A society in which people can vote for the leaders who will represent them in government

discriminatory Treating people unfairly based on their identity, such as their race, gender, or background

disproportionately Does not accurately represent a population; too large or small in comparison

ethnicities Groups of people who share common background, such as a national or cultural tradition

exaggerated To make something seem bigger, worse, or more significant than it really is

face value Describes something as it appears, without looking below the surface

feeds Broadcasts or sources of information, usually on websites

filter Sift through or sort based on criteria

global community All of the people who live on Earth

hate speech Criminal language that attacks a person or group based on their identity, such as their race

humanitarian crises Events or series of events that threaten the health or livelihood of a large group of people

implied To suggest something without stating clearly

industry Businesses that specialize in something specific, such as the film industry

informed Has knowledge and understanding about something

libel Written false statement that is damaging to a person's reputation

manipulative Describes an act that attempts to control someone or something

mass communication The passing of information among a large number of people

misinformation False or untrue information

outlets Media broadcast programs or publications

predetermined Previously decided

printing press A machine that prints text on paper

races Groups of people who share common physical characteristics, history, culture, and ancestors

restrictions Limiting conditions or measures

slander Spoken false statement that is damaging to someone's reputation

stereotypes Commonly held ideas of people or things that are too simple to describe them correctly

technical crew In a film, play, or musical performance; people who stay behind the scenes and control and operate technology such as cameras or lighting

transgender Describes a person whose gender does not match the sex they born with, or were assigned at birth

United Nations An international organization made up of 193 countries, meant to establish world peace and help solve global issues

unpatriotic Not showing love or respect to one's country

viral In the media; when something is shared and viewed a lot in a short amount of time

vloggers People who create blogs in video form

INDEX